The Black Girl's Guide to Calm

Printed in the United States of America

Dedication

Dedicated to my parents, for babysitting so I could finish this book and actually get work done. To my husband, Chris and daughter, Nailah for inspiring my new journey. To my mama and sister, for being my first unofficial meditation and yoga students. To my friends (social media included) and family for your support. Thank you all!

xoxo

Contents

A Brief History of My Journey to Here

Most people who know me – in real life and virtually– think that I'm this real chill, calm, laid-back person. And they'd be right (for the most part) if they were talking about me now. Beforehand? I was a stressed out, controlling, anxious, perfectionistic bundle of nerves. I might have been calm, cool and collected on the outside (that's the introvert in me, I think), but the inside was a totally different story. The only person who really knew the extent of my stress and worry was my husband, Chris.

When I think about it, I've been a perfectionist and somewhat anxious since I was a kid. Being the oldest, my parents expected me to be a great example to my sister, and because I naturally did well in school and loved going, As and Bs were expected, too. As I got older, I decided that I wanted to be in control of every detail in my life, so I became a planner, trying to plan every little thing to the tiniest detail. (Side note: There's nothing wrong with having a plan or vision for your life; you just have to remember that ultimately, it's not in your control so be flexible).

In high school, I started preparing for my future. My plan looked something like this:

- ☐ Graduate high school with honors (check)
- ☐ Go to college and graduate in four years (check)
- ☐ Get a "good job" (hmmm)

☐ Be a career woman living in the city in a
   fabulous apartment (uhhh...)

What is the saying? We plan, God laughs?
Fast forward to college, I met my then
boyfriend the first semester. By my sophomore
year, I'd changed my mind and decided that I *did*
actually want to get married, and I wanted him to
be my husband. The main issue was *he* didn't want
to get married and made that clear to me. However,
I truly believed at the time it would be too difficult
to find someone else to marry (this was around the
time the media started their "There's-a-Black-man-
shortage-and-Black-women-aren't-getting-
married" campaign") so he had to be it! While he is
a great person, he wasn't a good fit for me
relationship-wise, but I tried so hard to make it
work and get him to conform to the ideal I'd
created in my mind. Long story short, he and I
broke up, and I met my husband a short time after.
　　Chris and I married in 2011, and of course,
we've had our issues and ups-and-downs like all
marriages do. In the beginning, I remember
constantly feeling stressed and overwhelmed and
being so worried about money.
　　Again, I had a vision of this perfect life in my
head that just wasn't happening. I was always living
in the future, worrying about tomorrow. My worst-
case scenario never happened, so I was pretty much
worrying for nothing. Things always turned out
okay, but that didn't stop me from worrying the
next time a stressful situation popped up.

Fast forward to almost two years ago, we had our first child. Before having her, Chris and I talked about the new roles we'd each play. I'm a work-at-home entrepreneur, while he works 12 hours a night, six to seven days a week. I was cool with doing the majority of the housework since he works such long hours and clutter drives me crazy. However, when I had Nailah, I knew I would need him to help out more because obviously, taking care of another human being, in addition to everything else I'd have going on, would be a whole 'nother ball game.

Things, once again, didn't work out the way I'd envisioned. For the first few months of Nailah's life, I was incredibly frustrated, disappointed, and depressed. And on top of that, I felt guilty about my feelings.

The tension between us became thick, and it was a pretty rough time. I finally got tired of feeling the way I did, so I decided to do something about it. To start, I journaled, I prayed, and I wrote some affirmations on how I wanted to feel.

I also began working out (partially to get back in shape and partially because I wanted to be a good example to Nailah by taking care of myself), and that helped with my stress. I started with Blogilates, then I (re)started doing yoga, which I kind of became obsessed with in early 2015. I read yoga blogs and books, pored over photos of yogis on Instagram, and participated in challenges. Yoga not only helped me de-stress, I also learned how important my breath is and how to utilize it, and it led me to learning more about meditation. I'd been meditating off and on for a few years, but earlier this year I committed to making it a part of my daily life.

Both yoga and meditation have been life-changing along with the other find-your-calm methods I share in this book. I am now more positive, much happier, and more peaceful.

And the experiences that led me to this moment have taught me a couple of powerful lessons:

1. I can only ever deal with the present moment because that's where I am. Sure, I can learn from my past and plan for my future, but I don't live in the past, and I don't live in the future. Instead of fretting about what I'm going to do tomorrow, I have to focus on what I can do right now;

2. I'm not in control. Even though, logically, I've always known that God is ultimately in control, that didn't stop me from trying to make things happen how I thought they should. That's not to say we don't have a part in making things happen in our lives. What I *am* saying is you do what you can to create the life you want, then let God figure out everything else.

Why Black Girl's Guide to Calm?

I decided to create Black Girl's Guide to Calm and this book for a few reasons: 1) I'm a Black woman whose purpose is to inspire and empower other Black women; 2) I believe that Black women are one of the most stressed out groups of people in this country and need to learn ways to stress less and find calm (it's literally a life-or-death situation for some of us); and 3) I've learned to find more calm in my life, to live in the moment, and have more joy. I want to show women like me how they can do the same.

So, take some time for yourself, and get ready to learn how you can find your calm!

Chapter 1
What You Need to Know About Stress

"Stress is not what happens to us. It is our response to what happens. And response is something we can choose."- Maureen Killoran

According to the American Psychological Association, stress is "the physiological demand placed on the body when one must adapt, cope, or adjust." While stress can be healthful and is necessary in keeping you alert, too much or continuous stress can wreak havoc on your body.
Negative effects of stress include:
- Feeling angry, hostile, irritable, or anxious
- Moodiness and feeling frustrated with things that don't usually bother you
- Sadness
- Upset stomach, headache, and backache
- Difficulty sleeping
- Over- or under-eating

Two of the major types of stress are acute and chronic:
Acute stress is the most common. It's short-term and comes from the demands and pressures of the recent past and the expected demands and pressures of the near future.

Chronic stress is long-term. It develops from continuous feelings of hopelessness as a result of things like poverty, family dysfunction, feelings of helplessness, and/or traumatic early childhood experience. Chronic stressors associated with health inequalities include discrimination (perceived and actual), and neighborhood, daily, family, acculturative, environmental, and maternal stresses.

More findings:

- Perceived discrimination (i.e. work place, gender-, race/ethnicity-, and sexual orientation-based) has been found to be a key factor in chronic stress-related health disparities with ethnic/racial and other minority groups.

- African-Americans, Native Hawaiian, and Latino-Americans have been impacted greatly by hypertension and diabetes due to chronic stress resulting from discrimination.

- Perceived discrimination/racism has been shown to play a role in behaviors like cigarette smoking, alcohol/substance use, improper nutrition, and refusal to seek medical services; it has also been shown to contribute to mental health disorders among groups like Asian-Americans and African-Americans.

- Acculturative stress refers to the feeling of tension and anxiety that follows efforts to conform to mainstream culture. This type of stress can have an influence on physical and mental health causing hypertension and depression.

- The Sojourner syndrome and the Superwoman Schema (SWS) concepts are used to explain the occurrence of early onset dis-ease of African-American women in response to constant chronic stress and active coping associated with meeting day-to-day demands and having multiple caregiver roles.

How Stress Affects You Physically

When you're in a stressful situation, your body responds with the fight-or-flight response: Your heart beats faster and harder, preparing you to either fight or run away. This causes your coronary arteries to constrict, and your brain causes other organs (such as the adrenal glands) to secrete stress hormones like adrenaline; stressful situations also causes steroids like cortisol, which circulate in the blood until they reach your heart.

If you find that you're always stressed out and overwhelmed:

- You could be causing tension, anxiety, and/or depression.
- There could be more blood clots in your arteries, reducing the blood flow to your heart.

- The arteries in your heart could constrict, causing spasms. And when a coronary artery goes into spasm, it can injure the lining of the artery, leading to cholesterol deposits and plaque build-up.
- You could be developing chronic high blood pressure.
- Constant stress can also weaken your nervous and immune systems.

Now that you understand how too much or the wrong kind of stress can negatively affect your well-being, let's talk about ways you can lessen it in your daily life.

Chapter 2
Meditation + Breathing

"Within yourself is a stillness and a sanctuary to which you can retreat anytime." – Herman Hesse

As I mentioned in the introduction, I started meditating consistently earlier this year. As I began practicing yoga on a regular basis, I wanted to learn more about it, so I spent a lot of time researching and reading yoga blogs. One of the sites I found was DoYouYoga.com, and on there, I found a 30 Day Meditation Challenge with Faith Hunter, a global yoga instructor. Through participating in and completing the challenge, I discovered how beneficial and transformational it was for me to simply sit in silence at least once a day. I felt like a different woman!

The shift I experienced gave me the desire to share the beauty of meditation with others, so I decided to become a certified meditation teacher.

If you're not familiar with meditation, you might think that you have to "be good at it" to practice, that you don't have time for it, or that meditation is only for certain types of people.

None of the above assumptions are true. There's no such thing as being good at meditation. Whether you only have two minutes or two hours; whether you're a 16-year-old Black girl, a creative freelancer, or an account manager in Corporate America, meditation is for you. Meditation is for everybody!

What is meditation?

Meditation has several definitions, but we'll go with this one: "a precise technique for resting the mind and attaining a state of consciousness that is totally different from the normal waking state."

When you meditate, your mind is relaxed and inwardly focused. You're fully awake and alert, but your mind isn't concentrating on what's going on around you. Meditation requires your inner state to be still and one-pointed so that your mind becomes silent; when your mind is silent and is no longer a distraction, your meditation practice deepens.

This deepening doesn't necessarily happen the first, second, third, 15th (you get the point) time you meditate. **Meditation is a practice,** meaning that if you want to reach that deeper level and reap the benefits, you have to do it consistently.

Additionally, by practicing meditation, you can ultimately train your mind to stop identifying with thoughts that cause you to respond to stressful situations in your life. When you stop identifying or becoming mixed with any particular thought or physical sensation, the space behind your thought – your true self, which is always peaceful – is experienced.

As you become more aware through stillness and quiet, you'll see that some thoughts create more stress because they lead your attention towards worry, doubt, and fear. Through meditation, you're better able to keep the positive thoughts you have and release the negative ones. You don't have to stop the flow of these thoughts, though; just do your best not to identify with or dwell on them.

Meditation also helps when it comes to changing your mindset from negative to positive. Since I've started meditating consistently, I've become a lot more conscious of the thoughts I think. Being more aware of what I think allows me to redirect my thoughts when they're negative and not serving me.

Why You Should Meditate

In addition to helping you change your mindset, here are some other ways meditation benefits you:

- Meditation reduces stress and reverses the flight-or-fight reaction.
- It creates a sense of inner peace and calm.

- It strengthens your immune system and reduces cardiovascular problems and chronic pain.
- Meditation stimulates creativity.
- It increases job satisfaction.
- Meditation decreases your tendency to worry.
- It helps you keep things in perspective.
- It brings your mind, body, and spirit in harmony.
- Meditation helps you live in the present moment.

Preparing for Meditation

Almost anything you do can be meditation (more on that later), but if you want to meditate in the traditional way, first find a quiet place that's distraction-free. It can be in your bedroom, your living room, or the bathroom if that's the only place you can get away to; just use what you've got. You can sit on the floor (or your yoga mat if you have one), if that's comfortable for you. If not, sit in a chair or on your bed.

What to do with your hands

A few ways you can position your hands when meditating:

- Place the back of your hands on your knees or thighs with your palms facing up or facing down.
- Put the backs of your hands on your knees or thighs with your palms facing up, and bring your index fingers and thumbs to touch.
- Place your hands together like you're praying and bring it to the middle of your chest.
- Put your hands in your lap, palms facing up with one on top of the other and your thumbs touching.

How to Sit

However you choose to sit when meditating, make sure that your back is straight and that your body is as relaxed as possible. With each inhale, feel your spine growing taller, and with each exhale, feel yourself becoming more grounded.

You can sit are with your legs crossed (as the kids say, "Criss cross, apple sauce"); kneel, using a cushion if you need to; or in quarter, half, or full lotus. Alternatively, you may want to sit with your back against a wall for support or sit on a pillow or blanket. If you're sitting in a chair, place your feet firmly on the ground. (You can see examples of these at bit.ly/BGCfree).

You can add to your peaceful environment by lighting a candle, burning incense, or turning on some chanting or instrumental music.

How long to Meditate

Some long-time meditation practitioners meditate for an hour a day; those who practice Transcendental Meditation meditate 20 minutes twice each day; others practice five or 10 minutes twice a day. If you're a beginner, I suggest starting with five minutes two times a day (in the morning and in the evening), then work your way up to longer times.

Using an app like Meditation Helper or Calm can help you meditate a certain amount of time without you having to watch the clock or worry if your time is up. Both allow you to customize the length of your meditation and lets you know when it's over with a soft bell.

How to Meditate

Two types of meditations you can use are concentration and mindfulness.

With concentration meditation, you focus on a single point. You can concentrate on your inhalations and exhalations (I sometimes like to inhale and exhale while counting to four or eight, making them of equal length), repeat a single word or mantra, or gaze at a non-moving object. When you notice your mind wandering, gently bring your awareness back to the chosen object of attention and let the thought go.

Mindfulness meditation encourages you to observe your wandering thoughts as they drift through the mind. The intent is to not get involved with the thoughts nor judge them but to simply be aware of them and let them float on by.

Finally, when it comes to your meditation practice, don't worry so much about how well it is or isn't working. If you just let whatever happens happen, you'll benefit more. Worrying about your meditation practice will cause the stress response, the opposite of the relaxation response, which is what you don't want. Also, know that there is no perfect way to meditate. Some days, it'll come easy to you; other days, you won't want to do it, you won't be able to tame your monkey mind, and you'll wonder if meditating is worth the trouble. It is. Just keep practicing, and you'll ultimately reap the benefits and notice how it's changing your life.

Why the Way You Breathe Matters

If you pay attention, you'll notice that your breath is closely linked with your emotions. When you're calm or content, your breath is deep and slow. When you're tense, angry, anxious, or fearful, your breath is either held in or it becomes irregular, short, or difficult. Accordingly, when you change your breathing pattern, you can better manage your emotions and feel calmer.

Breathing Techniques for Finding Calm

Deep Abdominal Breathing

The most common way to breathe when meditating — and how you should actually breathe all the time — is deep abdominal breathing.

Here's how to do it:
1. Inhale and puff out your abdomen.
2. Gently bring the breath up, allowing it to go up through your rib cage, your sides, then continue bringing your breath up, expanding to your chest.
3. Slowly begin exhaling the breath to reverse the process. Exhale from the chest, allowing the rib cage and the abdomen to gently go down, back toward your spine.

Try it now by taking five slow, deep breaths. Notice the difference in how you feel?

Deep abdominal breathing reverses the stress reaction by providing more oxygenation of the blood. It helps you relax more, provides better emotional balance and control, greater mental clarity, and it improves your health in general.

Alternate-Nostril Breathing

This is another breathing technique you can use when meditating or when you need to decompress. Alternate-nostril breathing helps soothe, purify, and strengthen your nervous system, and it helps you develop control of your body, mind, and emotions. It also helps increase mental alertness, cleanses and opens your nasal passages, and combats the side effects of stress.

Here's how to do it:
1. Make a gentle fist with your right hand, extend your thumb and last two fingers, leaving space for your nose.
2. With your thumb, close off your right nostril and exhale through your left one.
3. Using deep abdominal breathing, inhale through your left nostril, close it off with your last two fingers, then exhale through your right nostril.
4. Continue by inhaling through your right nostril, closing it off, and exhaling through your left.
5. Repeat, alternating between right and left nostrils.

To get audios of these breathing techniques (including progressive deep relaxation), go to bit.ly/BGCfree.

Chapter 3
Using Affirmations & Mantras to Find Your Calm

"An affirmation is almost like a mantra. It does not really matter if what you are affirming is not totally true as yet. By repeating an affirmation over and over again, it becomes embedded in the subconscious mind, and eventually it becomes your reality." – Stuart Wilde

A mantra is a "sound, word, or phrase that is repeated by someone who is praying or meditating." (Merriam-Webster) The word mantra has two parts: *man*, the root of the Sanskrit word for mind; and *tra*, the root of the word instrument. "A mantra is therefore an instrument of the mind, a powerful sound or vibration that you can use to enter a deep state of meditation." (Chopra.com)

A couple of examples of ancient mantras are *Om* and *Isis*. Om is said to be a sound from the beginning of time, representing everything and is believed to be the seed of all creation. (YogiTimes.com) You pronounce it like "home" without the h...*oooommmm*.

Isis is the Egyptian goddess of rebirth and the personification of the "complete female." (GoddessGift.com). The I is pronounced like a long e (like in the word "eagle"), and the s is a hiss (ssss) ... *iiiiisssss*. When using this mantra, take a breath between each syllable.

Additionally, you can create your own mantras for meditating. Here are five I use:

1. I am calm and centered.
2. I am open to receive.

3. Breathe in courage, exhale fear.
4. Prosperity flows to me; prosperity flows through me.
5. The peace of God shines through me.

Ways you can use mantras include:
- Repeat it silently to yourself.
- Repeat it and notice the quiet space between each repetition of the mantra.
- Say the mantra while counting. You can use a set of mala beads, and on each repetition, move to the next one; or you can count the number of beads aloud.
- Repeat your mantra out loud. This is known as chanting and can assist you in becoming relaxed and focused. It can also enhance your silent meditation, which can follow the chanting.

Using Affirmations for Calm

I think the first time I heard about affirmations and how they work was in 2007. I was completing an internship at a domestic violence shelter and living with my cousin for the summer in Athens, GA. In addition to working at the shelter, interns also worked at the shelter's thrift store. So I often went to the library to kill time before going to work at the store. I picked up a book by Iyanla Vanzant; I can't remember which one, but I do remember that I learned about affirmations from it.

From there, I've read many books about using affirmations, visualizing, and the Law of Attraction in general. Using these techniques has created a positive change in my life, and I've also come to realize that using affirmations is a powerful way to relieve stress in your life.

According to success coach and co-author of the "Chicken Soup for the Soul" series Jack Canfield, an affirmation is a statement of your goal or desire now realized in the present time. They are statements you can write down then repeat regularly so you bombard your subconscious mind with the thoughts, images, and feelings you would be experiencing if your goal was complete already.

To make your affirmations effective, do the following:

1. Begin with the words "I am," and/or use present tense. You want to speak your statement as if it's already happening *right now*.

2. Make it positive. For example, instead of saying, "I don't let negative people disturb my peace," say, "I am only allowing positive people around me, and that gives me peace."

3. Keep it short.

4. Be specific.

5. Make them for yourself. Making affirmations for or about others doesn't work because the other person has to want it for herself or himself. Remember, you can only control *you*.

Once you've created your affirmations (or if you find some that resonate with you in a book or online), try to read them twice a day (in the morning when you get up and right before you go to bed are great times); if possible, read them out loud; and try to create the feeling of peace and calm you'll have when your affirmations are your reality.

Other Ideas for Using Affirmations
- Write them on index cards and post them around your home.
- Repeat your affirmations during down time, like if you're waiting in line, running, or driving.
- Record your affirmations (or have a loved one do it for you), and listen to them while you're working, exercising, driving, or falling asleep.
- Make them your screensaver on your computer, tablet, and/or phone.

Visualizing Your Way to Peace
Visualization is another great technique you can use to create more calm in your life because your brain doesn't know the difference between you visualizing something and that something being a reality.

Here's how it works:

Visualization activates the creative power of your subconscious mind. It focuses your brain by programming its reticular activating system (RAS) to notice available resources that have always been there but went unnoticed.

It also magnetizes and attracts you to the people, resources, and opportunities you need to achieve your goal. When you constantly visualize your goals as complete, it creates conflict in your subconscious mind between what you're visualizing and what you currently have. Your subconscious mind then works to resolve this conflict by turning your current reality into your new vision.

When the conflict is intensified over time by your constant visualization, three things happen:

1. It programs your brain's RAS to start helping you become aware of anything in your life that will help you achieve your goals.

2. It activates your subconscious mind to create solutions for accomplishing your goals, and you'll find yourself having new ideas everywhere, all the time: in the shower, driving, cooking, etc.

3. It creates new levels of motivation. You'll start to notice that you're unexpectedly doing things that take you to your goal. When you give your brain specific, colorful, and vividly compelling pictures to manifest, it will seek out and capture all the necessary info to bring that picture into reality for you.

How does this work for creating calm?

You've probably heard about and might even practice visualizing for other desires like a romantic relationship, more business, or more money. You can also use this technique for more calm and peace in your life.

One way to visualize more calm in your life is to close your eyes, breathe deeply, and imagine yourself being bathed in a golden light. Start from the top of your head and imagine it coming down, covering your entire body until you get to the soles of your feet while visualizing each part of your body relaxing. Feel the energy and the peace from the light.

Here's another technique to try:

1. Find a quiet, distraction-free space (if possible), and make yourself comfortable.
2. Close your eyes, and take a few deep breaths to center yourself.
3. Imagine yourself in a beautiful location where everything is as you'd ideally have it. I like to visualize myself on a quiet beach.
4. Visualize yourself calm and relaxed, and/or imagine yourself smiling and feeling happy.
5. Focus on the different sensory aspects, making it more vivid in your mind. For example, going with the beach scenario, imagine feeling the sun's warmth on your skin, smelling the salt from the ocean, and hearing the sound of the waves and sea gulls. The more you can involve your senses in this

exercise, the more realistic the entire image will become.

6. Remain with your scene, taking in the various sensory features for five to 10 minutes or until you feel relaxed.

Open your eyes, and rejoin your world.

How do you feel?

Chapter 4
Self-Care + Creating Routines

"Rest and self-care is so important. When you take time to replenish your spirit, it allows you to serve others from the overflow. You cannot serve from an empty vessel." – Eleanor Brownn

After becoming a mama back in 2013, I realized how important it is to take care of myself. And I'm sure you can relate on some level. With all the roles and responsibilities we have as women, it can be difficult to find – or should I say make – time for ourselves. But what I've learned is that while people love and care about you, they probably aren't going to make sure that you make you a priority. You have to do that yourself, or it won't happen. You also have to learn that you can't give to and care for your family, friends, clients, etc. if you're depleted with nothing left to give.

I learned this the hard way after burning out a few times and just feeling extremely frustrated with how things were going in my life. I now know that if I don't make sure I'm taken care of – spiritually, mentally, emotionally, and physically – I can't do my best at anything. So, I've made a commitment to putting myself first and taking care of me.

Chris works at night, so if Nailah decides to get up when I do, and I don't get to meditate and have my time right when I wake up, I'll wait until he gets there to do so, and I'll also practice yoga. If I'm not feeling well (I have migraines) or if I'm super tired, I'll get Chris to wake up a little earlier so I can take a nap. And since she's older, Nailah spends the night with my parents once or twice a week so I can get more work done (have you tried working with a rambunctious toddler at home?) or just have a little time to myself. By creating these small pockets of time for myself, I find that I'm much more at peace and am better able to handle the curve balls throughout the day.

If you have children, you may not have the luxury of your kids' grandparents babysitting. Or maybe you're a single parent, doing it by yourself. If either of these is your situation, see if there's a friend, co-worker, or trusted teen who can babysit for a few hours. You might also consider hiring a babysitter or exchanging child care services with another woman (or group of women) so you have that time to yourself.

Whatever your situation and whether you have children or not, there are ways to make time to take care of you. Some ideas:

- Create a weekend ritual. If you don't have a whole lot of time during the week, do something for yourself on the weekends. For example, this could be your time for giving yourself a facial and deep conditioning your hair.
- Meet a friend for coffee or a meal.

- Watch a movie you've been wanting to see.
- Smile.
- Take yourself out on a date.
- Write a list of things you love about yourself or of your successes, and keep it handy for when you need it.

Creating Routines for Calm

Another way you can make self-care a priority is to create morning and evening routines.

Having a routine you complete every morning helps set the tone for a productive, calm, and overall more successful day.

I've found that when I do certain things right after I wake up, I feel a lot better mentally and emotionally during the day. That's not to say that everything goes perfectly and according to my plans, but when things do veer off course, I handle them better. I also feel more calm and ready for what the day will bring, and I can definitely tell the difference in how I feel when I complete my routine versus when I don't.

Morning Routines

Here's my morning routine for most days: I usually wake up between 6:00 and 6:30, and I thank God for a new day. Then, I take Nailah, who's usually sleeping, with me in the kitchen so I can fix my breakfast of two whole grain waffles with natural peanut butter, and I go back to the bedroom. While I'm eating, I read something inspirational and my affirmations, and sometimes, I look at my Pinterest vision board and my physical one, which lives by the bed. I try to get my meditation in before Nailah wakes up as well, but as I mentioned, if I'm not able, I wait until Chris gets home, or I'll wait until she takes a nap. If I have to wait, I take a few deep breaths to center myself. Finally, I set an intention for the day, whether it's to stay present, focus on one thing at a time, or to go with the flow of my day.

Of course, you don't have to wake up at the crack of dawn, unless that's your thing, and you don't have to do what I do. You should create a routine that works for *you* and your lifestyle. I do, however, suggest the following:

- When your eyes pop open (or your alarm goes off), feel excited and express thanks for a new day.
- Don't pick up your phone and get on Facebook, Twitter, Instagram, etc.
- Meditate, if possible. If not, take a few deep breaths to center yourself.

- Set an intention for how you want to be and feel during your day.
- Read something inspirational. It could be a book, blog post, scripture, or a quote.
- Read or recite affirmations so you can set the tone for an amazing day.
- Try to be consistent with your routine, no matter what. I do have days when I don't feel like doing my routine, and I feel like I could be doing something more productive. But like I mentioned, my days just aren't the same without it. If you do happen to skip it one day (or a few), don't beat yourself up. Just get back on track the next morning.

Evening Routines

Having a consistent night routine is, I have to admit, something I still struggle with. I work from home with a toddler, so many of my work-related tasks get done after Nailah goes to sleep, and many nights, by the time I shut things down, I'm too tired to do anything but read a little, scroll on Instagram then fall asleep. However, I'm working on it because I know it's important to wind down before going to bed.

One of the main reasons to maintain an evening routine is so you can get as good a night's rest as possible so you'll be energized and ready for the next day.

These are the activities I try to do before going to sleep:

- Stop working at least 30 minutes before going to bed. I've read that you should stop working and shut all electronics down an hour before bed. However, if you're an entrepreneur, you might work at night, too, so this might prove to be a bit difficult. I do believe there should be some downtime between when you stop working and when you go to sleep. Whether it's 10 minutes, 30 minutes, or an hour is up to you.

- Write my intentions list for the next day. Also known as a to-list, doing this prepares me for the next day. It helps me maintain focus so I'm not wondering what I need to do or just jumping from one task to the next with no direction.

- Journal. This one is off and on, but I'm working on writing in my journal at least once a week because it helps me process my thoughts, feelings, and emotions about what's going on in my life

- Meditate. I try to do this at least five minutes, ideally 10.

- Read my affirmations and goals (and some nights, visualize). For me, nighttime is when my mind starts to wander. I start overthinking, and sometimes, fearful, negative thoughts try to creep in. Reading my affirmations and goals and visualizing helps me focus on something positive so I can fall asleep more easily, and it also allows something good to be put into my subconscious mind.

- Read a devotional and/or a book. This is another way for me to keep my mind on something positive.
- Write in my gratitude journal. I write down at least five things I'm thankful for that happened during my day.
- Pray.

Chapter 5
Everyday Mindfulness

"Mindfulness is about being fully awake in our lives. It is about perceiving the exquisite vividness of each moment. We also gain immediate access to our own powerful inner resources for insight, transformation, and healing." – Jon Kabat-Zinn

"Mindfulness means being awake. It means knowing what you are doing," says Jon Kabat-Zinn, Professor Emeritus and creator of the Stress Reduction Clinic and the Center for Mindfulness in Medicine, Health Care, and Society at the University of Massachusetts Medical School.

When practicing mindfulness, not only are you aware of the present moment, you're also in a state of emotional non-reactivity, meaning no matter how good or bad the experience, you don't judge it. Or if you do judge it, you just observe your thoughts with a friendly interest, and then you release them. You simply accept whatever is happening in the moment.

Being a society of multitaskers (and being women in particular), practicing mindfulness can be a little challenging. We all have so much going on, and we're trying to get it all done. But the benefits of having more peace and being more productive are worth the effort.

Here are tips for being more mindful from Leo Babauta of ZenHabits.net:

1. **Do one thing at a time.** Instead of multitasking, single-task. A Zen proverb says: "When walking, walk. When eating, eat."
2. **Do it slowly and deliberately.** Instead of rushing a task, take your time and do it slowly. It takes practice to be conscious of your actions instead of them being rushed and random, but doing things slowly helps you focus on the task at hand.
3. **Do less.** If you do less, you can do the things you do more completely and with more concentration. If you fill your days with a bunch of to-do's, you'll be rushing from one thing to the next without stopping to think about what you're doing. You might think you're too busy to do less, but it's possible. It's just a matter of figuring out what's really important and letting go of what's not.
4. **Put space between things.** Related to the above tip, this is a way of managing your schedule so you always have time to complete each task. Instead of scheduling to-do's close together, leave room between things; this will give you a more relaxed schedule, and it'll leave space in case one task takes longer than you anticipated.
5. **Spend at least five minutes a day doing nothing.** Just sit in silence, and become aware of your thoughts. Focus on your breath, and notice the world around you. Become comfortable with silence and stillness. It'll do you a world of good.

6. **Stop worrying about the future; focus on the present.** Start becoming aware of your thoughts: Are you constantly worrying about the future? Learn to recognize when you do this, and when it happens, practice bringing yourself back to the present moment. As much as possible, focus on what you're doing right now. Enjoy the moment you're in.

7. **When speaking with someone, be present.** How often does this happen with you: You're spending time with someone, but you're thinking about what you need to do later on. Or, you're thinking about what you want to say next instead of really listening to the person talking. Focus on being present, really listening and enjoying your time with the person.

8. **Eat slowly and savor your food.** Food can be shoved down our throats in a hurry, but there's no joy in that. Savor each bite, slowly, and really get the most out of your food. A bonus: You'll eat less and digest your food better.

9. **Live slowly and savor your life.** Just like you'd savor your food by eating it more slowly, do everything this way – slow down and savor every moment.

10. **Make cooking and cleaning meditation.** These tasks are often seen as drudgery (especially when you do them all the time), but they're both actually great ways to practice mindfulness. If cooking and cleaning are boring chores to you, try completing them as a form of meditation by putting your whole mind into them, concentrating and doing them slowly and completely. Not only can it change your entire day, it'll also leave you with a cleaner space.
11. **Keep practicing.**

How can you be more mindful today?

Chapter 6
Enjoy Your Journey

"Comparison is an act of violence against the self." –
Iyanla Vanzant

A little over a year ago, I took a break from Facebook. One reason was that I'd been checking it entirely too much for no reason and wasting time; another was that I found myself feeling a little envious of some of my other entrepreneur friends and feeling down about the progress I was making. Or, as I felt, the lack thereof.

And can I keep it real with y'all? I *still* have brief moments like that from time to time when I'm on Facebook or Instagram. Because most people only share the best parts of their lives (and there's nothing wrong with that; I do the same), it's easy to get caught up in how much better we think someone else's life is, even if we know they're only presenting the highlights.

Focusing on and worrying about what the next person is doing can cause anxiety and negative feelings, and it can stress us out, trying to figure how they did it and why we didn't do it and how we can do what they did. How can we be at peace with who we are now and become the best versions of ourselves with those feelings swirling around? *We can't.*

We have to remember to focus on our own journeys and realize that life isn't a competition. Wherever you are right now is exactly where you're supposed to be. And besides, there is more than enough abundance for all of us to partake, so you don't have to think that another sista is taking something from you – she's not. Be happy for her, and focus on being the best you that you can be and make sure you enjoy the journey.

When these feelings come up (and they will because we're human), here's what you can do:

1. **Take a minute.** Log off, and take a few deep breaths to center yourself. You might also want to say a few affirmations, reminding yourself of how great you are. You might even want to write down some of your accomplishments (and put them up for other moments like this).

2. **Remember that success doesn't happen overnight.** A lot of times, it seems that people become overnight successes, especially with social media. Truthfully, no one is a success overnight; it usually takes years. You have to keep in mind that you don't know the time, work, sweat, and tears someone has put in to attain their goals, which brings me to my next point...

3. **Don't compare!** Faceboook, Twitter, and other social media are often places that can lead to you feeling all kinds of yucky things: envy, overwhelm, inadequacy, and unworthiness just to name a few. It's *so* easy to get caught up in the comparison game and begin stressing about why we haven't done this or how we can do that. Theodore Roosevelt once said, "Comparison is the thief of joy." In other words, comparing yourself to other people leads to your joy (and I would say your peace too) being stolen. It's hard to be calm and happy when you're constantly worrying about what someone else is doing and trying to determine if you measure up. I've found that it helps to: a) Limit the amount of time you spend on social media (if this is an issue for you); b) Remember that you don't know what has gone on behind the scenes; and c) Know that your path is *your* path. We each get to where we're going in different ways and in various time frames, so just concentrate on *you*.

4. **Get inspired.** If you see another woman on social media who has accomplished something you want to achieve, you can ask her how she did it. If you have a relationship with her (if you're friends on social media), you can send her a short email or tweet her, letting you know how she's inspired you and ask if she has any advice. You can also read memoirs from successful women and draw inspiration from there.

5. **Focus on the positive.** Having an attitude of gratitude and focusing on the positive things happening in your life gives you more joy. And being appreciative sets you up for even better things to happen in your life. If you're having a difficult moment, take some time to write down all the things you're thankful for. Additionally, as mentioned earlier, create a gratitude journal where you write down things you're grateful for each night. Gratitude truly works wonder.

Focus on your journey, knowing that what's for you is and always be yours.

Chapter 7
Yoga for Stress Relief and Calm

"Anybody can breathe. Therefore anybody can practice Yoga." – T.K.V. Desikachar

I was introduced to yoga about seven years ago. As I cleaned and shelved donated items at the thrift store where I was working, I often browsed to see what I could find for myself. One day, I stumbled upon a yoga book that had basic poses, and I started doing them. After about a month or two, my practice pretty much dwindled.

At the end of last year, I decided that I wanted to take my yoga practice more seriously. And earlier this year, I discovered my current (virtual) yoga teacher, Yoga By Candace, and I've been doing her videos five to six days a week since January, plus some of her monthly Instagram challenges.

Through my practice, I've learned quite a few things including how to focus and why it's important; to keep breathing no matter what (on and off the mat); that progress takes time; and that yoga is a journey.

According to YogaJournal.com, the word yoga is from the Sanskrit word *yuj*, which means to yoke or bind and is often interpreted as "union" or "a method of discipline." Contrary to what you may believe or see online, yoga is much more than poses.

Pantanjali, the Indian sage, is believed to have gathered the practice of yoga into the Yoga Sutra about 2,000 years ago. A collection of 195 statements that serves as a philosophical guidebook for most of the yoga practiced today, The Sutra outlines eight limbs of yoga: the yamas (restraints); niyamas (observances); asana (postures); pranayama (breathing), pratyahara (withdrawal of senses); dharana (concentration); dhyani (meditation); and Samadhi (absorption).

Today, most people who practice yoga are practicing in the third limb, asana, a program of physical postures that was designed to purify the body and provide the physical strength and stamina needed for long periods of meditation.

Why Yoga?

In addition to things like increased flexibility and strength, yoga also:

Relieves stress. Yoga reduces the physical effects of stress on the body and has been known to reduce cortisol levels.

Helps you improve your breathing. Yoga includes breathing practices known as pranayama, which can be useful for reducing your stress response, improving lung function, and it encourages relaxation. Many pranayamas focus on slowing down and deepening the breath; this activates your body's relaxation response.

Connects you with the present moment. The more you practice yoga, the more aware you become of the world around you. It also helps you improve your focus, coordination, reaction time, and memory.

Cultivates inner peace and calm.

Yoga Poses for Stress Relief

While there are dozens of yoga poses that can help you de-stress, I want to share a few basic ones:

Child's Pose (Balasana)

Benefits of this pose:

- Gently stretches your lower back, hips, thighs, knees, and ankles
- Relaxes your spine, shoulders, and neck
- Increases the blood circulation to your head, which reduces headaches
- Massages your internal organs
- Calms your mind, helping relieve stress and tension

How to do it:

1. Start on your hands and knees.
2. Keep your knees hip-distance apart and your big toes touching. You can spread your knees a little wider for wide-legged child's pose variation if that's more comfortable.
3. Bring your hips back toward your heels (don't worry if your butt doesn't reach your heels). Your heart and chest should rest on

top of or between your thighs; rest your
forehead on the mat or floor.
4. Keep your arms long and extended with your
palms down on the ground. (You also have
the option to place your hands down by your
sides).
5. On your exhalations, allow any tension in
your neck, shoulders, and arms to melt away.

Legs-Up-the-Wall (Viparita Karani)

Benefits of this pose:

- Lessens anxiety and stress
- Is therapeutic for arthritis, high and low
  blood pressure, headaches, and insomnia
- Gently stretches the hamstrings, legs, and
  lower back
- Relieves lower back pain
- Calms the mind

How to do it:

1. Sit with your left side against the wall.
2. Gently turn your body to the left, then bring
   your legs up the wall.
3. Lay your back, head, and shoulders on the
   floor.
4. Shift your weight from side-to-side and scoot
   your butt close to the wall.

5. Open your arms on each side with your palms facing up.

Camel Pose (Ustrasana)

Benefits of this pose:

- Stretches your neck, chest, abdomen, thighs, hip flexors, groin, and ankles
- Strengthens your back, gluteal muscles and triceps
- Massages and stimulates your organs and chakras of the abdomen

How to do it:

1. Start by kneeling upright with your knees hip-distance apart. Press your shins and the tops of your feet into the floor.
2. Rest your hands on your lower back with your fingers pointing toward the floor. Slowly bend your back, letting your head come back if it's okay with your neck.
3. Stay there, or take the full expression of the pose by reaching back and grabbing a hold of the ankles or feet. Your palms should rest on your heels with your fingers pointing toward your toes and your thumbs holding the outside of each foot.

4. Keep your thighs in line with the floor with your hips directly over your knees.
5. After releasing, immediately come into Child's Pose so you don't get lightheaded or dizzy.

Corpse Pose (Savasana)

Benefits of this pose:
- Relaxes your central nervous system and calms your mind
- Helps relieve stress
- Relaxes your body
- Reduces insomnia and helps improve sleep
- Reduces headache and fatigue
- Helps relieve depression

How to do it
1. Lie on your back with your legs straight, mat-distance apart and your arms at your side. Rest your hands about six inches away from your body with your palms up.
2. Let your feet drop open to the sides, and close your eyes and your mouth (but part your teeth).
3. Working from the soles of your feet to the crown of your head, consciously release each body part, organ, and cell. Breathe naturally.

4. Relax your face, and let your eyes drop deep into their sockets. Invite peace and silence in.
5. To exit savasana, first start deepening your breath. Bring awareness back to your body by wiggling your fingers and toes. Roll to your right side and rest for a breath. Inhale, then use your left hand to gently press yourself into a comfortable seated position. Take a few deep breaths.

Seated Forward Bend (Paschimottanasana)

Benefits of this pose:
- Stretches your hamstrings, spine, and lower back
- Calms your mind and relieves stress and anxiety
- Improves digestion
- Relieves PMS and menopausal symptoms
- Reduces fatigue

How to do it
1. Sit up straight with your legs extended and toes pointed up to the sky. If you're a beginner (or your hamstrings are tight), you may want to bend your knees throughout the pose.

2. Inhale while reaching your arms out to the side, then up overhead and lengthen your spine by stretching.
3. Exhale and bend forward from your hip joints (not your waist). Lengthen the front of your torso by imagining your torso resting on your thighs.
4. Hold onto your shins, ankles, or feet – wherever you can grab. To help, you can use a towel or yoga strap around the soles of your feet. Keep your back flat instead of rounding it; it helps to focus your gaze a few feet in front of you instead of looking down.
5. With each inhale, lengthen your torso; and with each exhale, feel your belly getting closer to your thighs.

Tree Pose (Vrksasana)

Benefits of this pose:

- Stretches your inner thighs, groin, and shoulders

- Strengthens your posture and your thighs, calves, core, and foot muscles
- Helps you develop balance

- Calms and relaxes your mind and central nervous system
- Increases your mind/body awareness

How to do it

1. Stand tall and straight with your arms by your sides.

2. Bend your right knee and place your right foot high up on your left thigh or down on your calf (just make sure it's not on your knee). The sole of your foot should be flat and placed firmly wherever it is.

3. Keep your left leg straight, and find a non-moving eye-level point to gaze at. This will help you maintain your balance.

4. Once you're well balanced, inhale, and raise your arms overhead and bring your hands together in the 'prayer' position (you also have the option of keeping your hands chest-level).

5. Keep your eyes focused on the same object.

6. Make sure your spine is straight, and take full, deep breaths.

7. When you're ready to release, bring your hands down to your sides, then gently release your right leg.

8. Repeat on the other side.

To see video demonstrations of these poses, visit bit.ly/BGCfree.

A Few More Tips for Finding Your Calm from Some Amazing Women

"I [was] actually in a very stressful situation [recently]. My tire blew out on my way to Atlanta, so I was stuck in Dublin, [Georgia] for the night. How I find my calm, even in damning situations as this, is by looking past the ugh of what's going on and identifying what I actually can do to make myself feel better. [That night], that meant reserving this time to knock out some chapters in the book I'm writing. And of course, prioritizing self-care on a daily basis is my proactive choice in finding and maintaining my calm." – Trelani Duncan, Author and Writing Coach (SoFundamental.com)

"I find my calm by taking control where I can and releasing my grip in areas where control is just an illusion." – Tara Jefferson, Family Life Educator, Writer, and Founder of TheYoungMommyLife.com

"My go-to, never fails guide to calm is to concentrate on my breath. It's a trick taught to me to fight my fear of swimming in open waters. First, I acknowledge how I am breathing. It gives me a chance to reflect inward than [to] focus on the distraction or melee. Once I can control my breath to an equal pace of inhalations with an equal pace of exhalations, I assess the situation that caused me to lose my cool while practicing breath control. The process becomes meditative." – Janessa Mondestin, Holy Yoga Instructor, Holy Yoga NYC; Business Owner, Better Fit Body

"I find my calm by getting really present about what feels out of alignment. If I feel stressed about a particular project with a client, I stop working on it. I take time to feel through my feelings, and consciously decide how I need to shift my energy toward a better feeling. Sometimes that means writing it out. Other times it means getting on the phone with that client and talking about whatever's coming up. The route to finding my calm varies, but the catalyst for that calm can always be found in getting more present with my feelings." -Akilah S. Richards, Story Teller, Digital Nomad, Unschooler (RadicalSelfie.com)

25 More Ways to Find Your Calm

1. Ask for help (stop trying to be Superwoman).
2. Do a body scan to see if you're holding tension anywhere (if I am, it's usually in my shoulders), then relax.
3. Journal how you're feeling, how you want to feel and how you can get there.
4. Listen to music (India.Arie is usually my go-to).
5. Take a social media break.
6. Unplug and take a break from all technology.
7. Nap.
8. Say no.
9. Read.
10. Take a break.
11. Laugh.
12. Take a bubble bath or shower.
13. Color.
14. Play with your child (or someone else's).
15. Light a candle or two.
16. Exercise.
17. Get a massage.
18. Hang out with your pet.
19. Do something for someone else.
20. Kiss or hug someone.
21. Have sex.
22. Go for a walk or hang out in nature.
23. Paint your nails.
24. Go to bed early.
25. Pray.

15 Affirmations for Peace

1. As I exhale, all negativity is evaporating from my body and mind.
2. Every day, I feel more and more at ease.
3. Calmness washes over me with each deep breath I take.
4. I am relaxed in all situations.
5. I breathe in total peace and positivity; I exhale all stress and negativity.
6. I choose to experience life in a calm and peaceful manner.
7. I easily connect with my inner peace and quiet whenever I need to.
8. I handle any situation life throws at me in a calm and relaxed manner.
9. I maintain a calm and tranquil presence at all times.
10. With each breath, I bring more and more serenity into my life.
11. I focus on the now, and that brings me peace and joy
12. No matter what happens during my day, I remain calm and centered.
13. I remember to breathe throughout the day. I remind myself that I can choose peace, no matter what is going on around me. Whenever I desire, I can retreat to that quiet place within simply by closing my eyes. (ThoughtsforNow.com)
14. I choose to live in the present moment.
15. I accept the flow of life, and I freely release any attachment to the outcome. (A. Leigh Edwards)

Thank you

I hope you enjoyed this book and that you've learned how to create more calm in your life! If you have questions or comments, email me at hello@blackgirlsguidetocalm.com. Get more information, tips, and advice at BlackGirlsGuidetoCalm.com.

Don't forget to check out this book's resources: bit.ly/BGCfree

Also, follow #BlackGirlCalm online:
Facebook.com/Blackgirlcalm
Twitter.com/Blackgirlcalm
Instagram.com/Blackgirlcalm
(Youtube) bit.do/BGCalm

About the Author

Calm Coach Jamie Fleming-Dixon works with Black women who are tired of being burned out, stressed out, and worn out. She assists them in finding their calm through coaching services, products, and her blog, Black Girl's Guide to Calm.

Jamie's love of meditation and yoga was sparked after giving birth to her daughter, and she desires to teach women how to use the two, along with other tools, to create more calm and peace in the midst of all they have going on. She enjoys reading a good book and is kind of obsessed with nail polish. Jamie lives in Anderson, SC with her husband, daughter, and cat.

Made in the USA
Columbia, SC
08 May 2020

95455287R00036